TO MY DAUGHTER

with love

_____

_____

FROM

For My Daughter: There's No One Like You
Copyright © 2009 Hallmark Licensing, Inc.

Published by Hallmark Books,
a division of Hallmark Cards, Inc.,
Kansas City, MO 64141
Visit us on the Web at www.Hallmark.com.

Editorial Director: Todd Hafer
Editor: Megan Langford
Art Director: Kevin Swanson
Designer: Laura Rottinghaus
Production Artist: Dan Horton

ISBN: 978-1-59530-120-8

BOK4348

Printed and bound in China

FOR MY *daughter*
Karen

THERE'S NO ONE LIKE YOU

WRITTEN BY KEELY CHACE

GIFT BOOKS
from Hallmark

Karen

THERE'S NO ONE LIKE A DAUGHTER

TO MAKE *"love at first sight"*

SEEM LIKE A TOTAL UNDERSTATEMENT.

I'D SAY YOU HAD ME AT *hello*

BUT, OF COURSE, YOU COULDN'T TALK YET.

I WAS PRETTY speechless MYSELF

WHEN I LOOKED DOWN

AT THAT tiny bundle of you

IN MY SHAKY ARMS.

BUT YOU KNOW WHAT?

Over the years,

THE TWO OF US MORE THAN MADE UP

FOR THOSE FIRST QUIET MOMENTS.

AN EARLY MOMENT OF YOU

THAT I'LL ALWAYS REMEMBER IS . . .

THERE'S NO ONE LIKE A daughter

TO MAKE YOU wonder

HOW YOU USED TO SPEND ALL YOUR TIME.

WHAT ON EARTH

DID I DO WITH MY ARMS

BEFORE I HAD YOU TO HOLD?

IN OTHER WORDS, I WAS

certifiably gaga

OVER YOU.

THERE'S NO ONE LIKE A DAUGHTER

TO MAKE A MOM START

dreaming.

WHAT WOULD your life BE?

WHERE WOULD YOU GO?

WHAT WOULDN'T YOU DO?

I could hardly wait to see.

THERE'S NO ONE LIKE A DAUGHTER

TO ATTRACT *smiles* LIKE A MAGNET.

RIGHT FROM THE START,

YOU HAD THE WHOLE

irresistible THING DOWN.

WHEREVER WE WENT,

PEOPLE CAME OVER TO SAY

HOW pretty, HOW happy,

HOW special YOU WERE.

I COULDN'T HAVE AGREED MORE.

THERE'S NO ONE LIKE A DAUGHTER

TO MAKE TIME *fly.*

I SWEAR, ONE MINUTE

YOU WERE SITTING THERE

FLIRTING WITH THE IDEA OF CRAWLING . . .

. . . AND THE NEXT,

YOU WERE FLITTING AROUND

in fairy wings.

You just kept growing.

You became more and more
your own person every day.

You kept moving straight ahead

(with the occasional pause for a twirl).

And you taught me that sometimes

the best thing to do

is just sit back

and try not to miss anything.

ONE OF MY *favorite memories* OF YOU IS . . .

THERE'S NO ONE LIKE A DAUGHTER

TO GIVE YOU A *fresh perspective.*

Laundry, dusting, cooking . . .

BEFORE YOU,

I ACTUALLY THOUGHT

OF THOSE THINGS AS WORK.

TURNS OUT, ALL I NEEDED

WAS THE RIGHT HELPER.

THERE'S NO ONE LIKE A DAUGHTER

TO GIVE YOU THE PERFECT EXCUSE

TO DO YOUR FAVORITE *girl stuff*

ALL OVER AGAIN.

I DIDN'T DREAM OF BEING YOUR MOM

SPECIFICALLY SO I COULD TAKE UP

COLORING *princesses* AND

wishing on stars AGAIN.

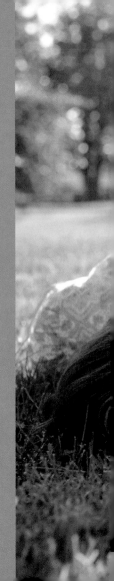

BUT YOU'LL NEVER

CATCH ME COMPLAINING

THAT THOSE THINGS TURNED OUT TO BE

PART OF THE DEAL.

Your joy MADE PINK

MY FAVORITE COLOR ALL OVER AGAIN.

WE STILL HAVE LOTS

OF FUN GIRL TIMES TOGETHER,

ESPECIALLY WHEN WE . . .

_____

_____

_____

_____

_____

_____

_____

THERE'S NO ONE LIKE A DAUGHTER

TO GET YOU *laughing.*

At first, it was the things you said.

Those *cute mispronunciations*

I secretly hoped

you'd never outgrow...

...and the grown-up-size

words that came out

of your *little-girl mouth*...

BUT THEN IT WAS YOUR SENSE OF HUMOR.

Before I knew it,

I WAS LAUGHING WITH YOU.

(A LOT.)

SOMETIMES I STILL LAUGH ABOUT THAT TIME YOU . . .

_____

_____

_____

_____

_____

_____

_____

_____

THERE'S NO ONE LIKE A DAUGHTER

TO MAKE YOU WISH

YOU HAD A FEW *superpowers.*

THE POWER TO GENERATE

A PROTECTIVE BUBBLE AROUND YOU

COMES TO MIND.

Part of me wanted to swoop in

AND RESCUE YOU

FROM EVERY SKINNED KNEE,

EVERY BROKEN HEART, EVERY TOUGH SITUATION . . .

But that wasn't what you needed.

Nope, *girl wonder,*

YOU JUST NEEDED A LITTLE SPACE

TO TRY OUT YOUR OWN POWERS.

AND, BELIEVE ME,

YOURS WERE DEFINITELY THE SUPER KIND.

THERE IS *so much* IT SEEMS

YOU WERE SIMPLY BORN TO DO.

AND I *love* WATCHING

YOU DO IT ALL.

There's no one like a daughter

TO REMIND YOU THAT THINGS

LIKE CONTACT LENSES AND PROM DRESSES

ARE HARDLY EVER FREE.

But you know what?

Seeing you smile that way

was *always* worth it.

THERE'S NO ONE LIKE A DAUGHTER

to bless you every day.

AND YOU GAVE ME so many blessings—

ESPECIALLY IN THOSE ORDINARY MOMENTS

WHEN I WAS LEAST EXPECTING IT.

A FEW OF THE WAYS YOU'VE BLESSED ME ARE . . .

THERE'S NO ONE LIKE A DAUGHTER

TO MAKE YOU *proud.*

There may have been times

when I asked if you were really planning

on wearing that.

(Sorry.)

But I can't remember a time

when I didn't feel like pointing you out

to anyone and everyone and saying,

"Look, there goes my daughter!"

THERE'S NO ONE LIKE A DAUGHTER

TO MAKE YOU STAND BACK

AND THINK *Wow*...

SOMEDAY, YEARS FROM NOW,

YOU'LL BE OLD AND GRAY

AND I'LL BE OLDER AND GRAYER ...

... BUT YOU'LL

still amaze me

EVERY DAY.

My heart will still fill up

at the sight of you

just being who you are.

And I'll still feel so lucky

to have you for a daughter.

THERE'S NO FRIEND LIKE

a daughter.

OF ALL THE SURPRISES YOU THREW MY WAY,

THAT MIGHT JUST BE MY FAVORITE.

I HAD MY SUSPICIONS . . .

. . . BUT I NEVER REALLY KNEW

WHAT *great friends* WE'D BE.

I didn't know THERE'D COME A DAY
WHEN WE'D START TALKING,
THEN LOOK UP AT THE CLOCK HOURS LATER,
WONDERING WHERE THE TIME WENT.

I couldn't have guessed THAT ONE DAY,
I'D BE ASKING FOR ADVICE FROM SOMEONE
I USED TO OVERHEAR TALKING TO HERSELF.

I LOVE SPENDING *time with you* BECAUSE . . .

How did I know we were friends? When did that part begin?

Maybe it was when you began asking me if I was really planning on wearing that.

Maybe it was when it dawned on me that I didn't just love you— I liked you.

ALL I KNOW FOR SURE IS THAT

LITTLE BY LITTLE,

WE DISCOVERED A CONNECTION THAT WAS

MORE *side by side,*

MORE *heart to heart.*

AND THAT'S SOMETHING

I'VE COME TO COUNT ON.

WE'LL ALWAYS HAVE

the mother-daughter thing.

BUT NOW WE HAVE THE FRIEND THING, TOO.

AND I LOVE THE FRIEND I'VE FOUND IN YOU.

THERE'S NO ONE LIKE A DAUGHTER.

Period.

Never, ever—

NOT IN A MILLION YEARS——

COULD I HAVE DREAMED UP ANYONE

QUITE LIKE YOU.

AND YET, SOMEHOW,
you're my dream come true.

YOU'RE EXACTLY THE DAUGHTER
I ALWAYS WANTED.

Exactly.

THERE'S NO ONE LIKE A DAUGHTER.

And there's no daughter like you.

(PLACE PHOTO HERE.)

A FEW OF THE GREAT THINGS

THAT MAKE YOU *you* ARE . . .

WHAT I LOVE MOST
ABOUT THE *daughter*
YOU ARE . . .

If you have enjoyed this book,

Hallmark would love to hear from you.

BOOKNOTES@HALLMARK.COM

BOOK FEEDBACK, HALLMARK CARDS, INC.
2501 MCGEE STREET, MAIL DROP 215
KANSAS CITY, MO 64108